Flaviana Aparecida de Mello

Domestic violence against women

Flaviana Aparecida de Mello

Domestic violence against women

An analysis of social aspects and social protection policy

ScienciaScripts

Imprint

Any brand names and product names mentioned in this book are subject to trademark, brand or patent protection and are trademarks or registered trademarks of their respective holders. The use of brand names, product names, common names, trade names, product descriptions etc. even without a particular marking in this work is in no way to be construed to mean that such names may be regarded as unrestricted in respect of trademark and brand protection legislation and could thus be used by anyone.

Cover image: www.ingimage.com

This book is a translation from the original published under ISBN 978-3-330-76020-2.

Publisher:
Sciencia Scripts
is a trademark of
Dodo Books Indian Ocean Ltd. and OmniScriptum S.R.L publishing group

120 High Road, East Finchley, London, N2 9ED, United Kingdom
Str. Armeneasca 28/1, office 1, Chisinau MD-2012, Republic of Moldova, Europe
Printed at: see last page
ISBN: 978-620-8-31531-3

SUMMARY

INTRODUCTION

In view of the discussions about the various forms of violence practiced against women, an important issue to be investigated is the understanding between domestic violence and acts of violence against women.

In the face of countless news reports about situations of violence faced by women in public places, for example on urban transport, the debate about what is meant by violence when it comes to women and what we have in the way of legal apparatus and public protection policies is drawing attention.

Although the term gender-based violence is recent, as is the recognition of the mistreatment of women, it is no longer possible to ignore this situation in Brazilian society.

Article 5 of the Brazilian Federal Constitution of 1988 emphatically proclaims equality between men and women. However, social images persist that men are superior to women in various dimensions.

Important declarations made at the World Conference on Human Rights held in Vienna in 1993, the 1994 Inter-American Convention to prevent, condemn and eradicate violence against women and, finally, the World Conference on Women held in Beijing in 1995 are highlighted throughout this work.

The resolutions adopted on these occasions can be seen as an expression of the resistance of women who recognize violence against them and question biological or even domestic explanations.

They treat it as a gender issue that results from a process of historical and social construction implying a set of social values, in other words, these values show and define the rules of behavior expected and practiced by men and women, even in contemporary societies.

Thus, it was up to men to occupy public spaces and women to remain in the private, domestic environment, with the responsibility of looking after the children, the husband and the responsibility of organizing the home.

These gender inequalities, i.e. between men and women, exalt the behavior of a manly man from birth. They are brought up to be strong and told not to show their emotions, for example, the phrase **"men don't cry!"** confirms this. Women, on the other hand, are given the role of fragility and therefore always need to be protected.

The differences between men and women take root in society based on conceptions of femininity and masculinity. These are symbolic disputes that concern the process of social reproduction, whether in the family, in religious organizations, at school, in the workplace, in political life and in the social division of labour.

In these social spaces, power practices and their mechanisms of subordination are configured, where the hierarchy of male over female gender is reinforced and naturalized, leading to unequal access for women and men in the various aspects of social and political participation.

Although much progress has been made, mainly due to the struggle and persistence of women organized through feminist social movements, in the face of the inequalities caused by gender issues, the various forms of violence and discrimination against women are still notorious.

One of the objectives of the work proposed here is to reflect on violence against women based on their own condition in society, its social aspects, to analyze important documents regarding the enforcement and guarantee of women's rights and finally to analyze what the Brazilian government has already provided in terms of legislation and social policies with programs focused on the issue of women, especially those who suffer violence.

Thus, this work is divided into four (4) chapters. Chapter I, entitled: The importance of understanding violence against women from the gender category and the relevance of the feminist movement in the fight to end violence against women, will cover the concept of gender, feminism and the importance of the feminist movement in the fight against violence against women.

Chapter II, titled: Violence against women: we can already put the spoon in, brings in the different forms of violence against women, typifies and presents each of them: gender violence, domestic violence and family violence, presents the phases of domestic violence, known as the "honeymoon cycle" and the other types of violence provided for in Law 11.340 of 2006 "Maria da Penha law" - physical violence, sexual violence, moral violence, property violence and psychological violence.

Chapter III contains a brief analysis of the social aspects of violence against women, where we briefly look at the social aspects of violence against women and also point out machismo.

And finally, chapter IV - treaty conventions and the Maria da Penha law - describes the Vienna and Inter-American conventions, among others. Its subtitle presents Brazilian social policies and mechanisms for dealing with violence against women.

The concluding remarks reflect on the entire development of this work and its relevance to a possible change in the way we look at women, as well as the need to achieve a less oppressive and macho way of educating from early childhood onwards.

CHAPTER I - THE IMPORTANCE OF UNDERSTANDING VIOLENCE AGAINST WOMEN FROM THE GENDER CATEGORY AND THE RELEVANCE OF THE FEMALE MOVEMENT IN THE FIGHT TO END VIOLENCE AGAINST WOMEN

1.1 - conceptualizing Gender

The concept of gender was created in the mid-1980s by feminists who sought to break with something that had historically been determined in society by the biological prism to refer to men and women.

It is important to note that this concept differentiates between the biological and the social. Sex determines differences between women and men biologically, while gender determines differences based on social and cultural relations.

According to Scott (1995), gender is understood as being constituted and maintained on the basis of norms, rules and social institutions that impose and define what is masculine and feminine, and therefore standardize the behaviour of women and men.

The category of gender is a social construction superimposed on a body, in other words, a significant form of domination and power. It is also worth highlighting the biological differences between women and men, which in many situations are used to reinforce discrimination and restrict women's autonomy and emancipation.

Saffioti (2004) appropriates the concept of patriarchy, which is understood through hierarchical relations between women and men and which expands through politics, education and culture.

It is important to point out that this concept discussed by Saffioti is present in our relationships in modern society, legitimizing women's subordinate status. This concept addresses the relationship of oppression of the male sex towards the female sex in order to gain economic, political and work advantages. As a result, all activities carried out by women are looked down upon and considered to be of lesser value in society.

Historically, men have been raised and educated for issues related to the outside world, the use of force, while women have always been educated to take care of the domestic unit, the husband and the children.

The differences between men and women take root in society based on conceptions of femininity and masculinity. These are symbolic disputes that concern the process of social reproduction, whether in the family, in religious organizations, at school, in the workplace, in political life and in the social division of labour.

Inequalities start from childhood. When we analyze how education is conducted and the ways in which girls and boys play and socialize, we realize that there is a differentiation that is rooted in and at the same time naturalized in the relationships established.

As soon as girls get their first toys, it becomes clear that they all refer to the idea of home, i.e. utensils that are used in a domestic unit such as: fridge, iron, broom, squeegee, stove, saucepans and so on.

Also noteworthy is the use of dolls resembling babies, where care must be taken to change clothes, bathe and breastfeed, symbolizing care for children.

When we look at boys' first toys, they are presented with dolls that have to be used with brute force, cars, soccer balls - none of these toys come close to actions that involve zeal and care.

It should also be noted that the behavior is totally different, with boys being told that they **"shouldn't cry"** while girls should be affectionate and delicate.

It is noticeable when we analyze that socially defined roles, passed down through generations, reinforce male domination in the face of women's inferiority. As Perrot points out

Women were created for the family and domestic matters. Mother and housewife, this is her vocation, and in this case she is beneficial to society as a whole. [...] Men are, in fact, the masters of the private sphere and, in particular, of the family, the fundamental, crystal instance of civil society, which they govern and represent, willing to delegate the management of everyday life to women (PERROT, 1998, p. 9-10).

Thinking about gender requires reflection and daily analysis by both men and women in order to construct and reconstruct roles that historically standardized what each person should assume and exercise in society.

We must understand that men are also somehow oppressed by these standards, because they are robbed of the right to learn and develop care and are restricted to the task of working and providing for their families.

1.2 - The importance of feminism in the study of violence against women

In order to understand the inequality between women and men, which is present in most societies, it is necessary to use the contributions of feminism.

Feminism as an intellectual current has several strands, aligning evaluations, discussions related to the issue of male domination over female domination and thus reinforcing resistance and the struggle for gender equality.

So we can understand that feminism can be defined by a critical construction that articulates the submissiveness of women in the domestic sphere and therefore excludes them from the public sphere.

1.3 - The emergence of feminism as a movement in the Western world

Feminism emerged as a political and intellectual movement at the end of the 18th century and the beginning of the 19th century, in the midst of the French Revolution. Miguel (2014) cites some women who took a stand to break down barriers and were important in the debate at the French Constituent Assembly: Théroigne de Méricourt and Olympe de Gouges, who presented the "declaration of the rights of women and citizens".

In the 19th century, utopian socialist feminism emerged, with Flora Tristan highlighting women as workers, linked to gender and social class oppression.

From the 20th century onwards, feminist struggles in the Western world really took off. In France, feminist women came together to fight for rights such as the vote, but it wasn't until the 1940s that they were able to enjoy this right.

In Brazil, the feminist movement began in 1919 under the name "Liga pela emancipaçâo intelectual feminina" (League for Women's Intellectual Emancipation) and in 1922 was renamed "Federaçâo Brasileira pelo Progresso Feminino" (Brazilian Federation for Women's Progress).

As the Brazilian feminist movement fought for equal rights, in 1930 women won the right to vote and in 1932 the president at the time, Getulio Vargas, created legislation to protect women's work.

For Saffioti (2013, p. 382)

The aspiration to liberate and emancipate oneself through work, a process that matured as female elements effectively entered areas that until then had been reserved exclusively for men.

However, in some ways women have made progress in certain areas, such as education, access to paid work and social life.

It's important to highlight the 1960s, which saw a very important factor not only for women in Brazil, but throughout the world: the discovery of the contraceptive pill, which could be understood as something in which women could decide whether or not to have children and the number of children they wanted to have. It also showed that women were not just reproducers, paving the way for discussion of the right to female sexuality.

We have to understand that during the feminist movement's struggle, at first it was about equal rights, which were denied to women, and then it began to question and debate the cultural and historical inequality between women and men based on biological determinism to justify the inferior treatment given to women.

At the height of the Brazilian military dictatorship, the Brazilian feminist movement was active and militant against the dictatorial government, and it is worth highlighting the arrests, torture and deaths of several women.

In the 1970s, the United Nations (UN) established March 8 as International Women's Day. This date alludes to the more than 100 women workers who were killed in a factory in New York, USA, for protesting in favor of rights such as maternity leave and a reduction in the long working day, which at the time was 14 hours a day.

However, what we see in the commemorations on this day is not the dissemination of the real meaning and significance, but rather the exaltation of the role of women as caretakers of the domestic unit, children and husband.

The same decade saw the start of the discussion on violence against women, which only became more widespread in the 1980s, gaining strength and becoming a central issue on the agenda of the Brazilian feminist movement.

It is understood that the Brazilian feminist movement at the end of the 1970s and beginning of the 1980s, in the midst of the democratic transition, collaborated in making public the discussion about equal rights for women and men, thereby seeking to achieve a place on the public policy agenda.

It should be noted that the promulgation of the 1988 Federal Constitution was a milestone for feminist movements, as it made it possible to win some rights for women.

In 1985, in the state of São Paulo, with all the struggle and militancy of the feminist movement, the first specialized women's police station (DEAM) was inaugurated.

As we enter the 1990s, the feminist movement is gaining ground and with it the emergence of non-governmental organizations (NGOs) that seek to act from the perspective of defending women's rights, corroborating with the creation of strategies to confront the violence suffered by women (REDE MULHER, 2012).

Discussions within the Brazilian feminist movement, based on violence against women and, consequently, on unequal gender relations, helped to secure specific legislation and specialized services for women's needs.

According to Simone de Beauvoir:

What they are demanding today is to be recognized as existing in the same way as men and not to subject existence to life, man to his animality. An existential perspective has therefore allowed us to understand how the biological and economic situation of primitive hordes should have led to the supremacy of males (BEAUVOIR, 1970, p. 86).

The Brazilian feminist movement understands that violence against women, especially by partners and ex-partners, takes place in the private domestic environment, a place that culturally and historically has been reserved for women, so in the next chapter we will list and address the concept of violence against women, as well as the various types of violence.

CHAPTER II - VIOLENCE AGAINST WOMEN - WE CAN ALREADY TAKE THE PLUNGE

To talk about violence against women, we must understand that this phenomenon exists in society historically, has deep roots in culture and is present in all social classes.

Chaui's (1985) definition of violence goes beyond the transgression of rules and norms and leads us to consider this issue from two other perspectives: the first is violence aimed at oppression, domination and exploitation in a relationship where difference and inequality predominate; the second is when conduct treats the other not as a human being, but as a "thing".

This contributes to disregarding the person's personality, ability to act and speak, placing them in a condition of passivity, inertia, in other words, another form of violence.

The topic of violence against women began to spread in the 1970s and, in the case of Brazil, gained greater strength in the 1980s. When researchers conducting feminist studies created this theme in order to understand not only the violence practiced against women in the domestic and family sphere, but also to evaluate and research violence beyond this space, thus understanding the public space as the locus of violence.

The relevance of this whole movement to the issue of violence against women was to problematize violence against women as something that violates women's human rights and, at the same time, to guarantee visibility so that it can be studied and debated in the field of law.

According to MELO and TELES (p.17, 2012), the expression violence against women was thus conceived "because it is practiced against women, simply because they are women".

For Souza (1996, p. 31), violence is "a phenomenon generated in social processes, which affects institutions, groups and individuals, being unequally distributed, culturally delimited and revealing the contradictions and forms of domination in society".

2.1 - The different forms of violence against women

In order to gain a better understanding of violence against women, it is necessary to look at concepts of violence.

Thus, according to MELO and TELES (p.13, 2012)

In its most frequent meaning, it means using psychological, intellectual and physical force to compel someone else to do something against their will, in order to constrain them, to curtail their freedom, thus preventing them from expressing their will.

This situation is manifested towards the other in such a way as to threaten, beat and even kill.

Article 1 of the Belém do Para Convention defines violence against women as any act or conduct based on gender that causes death, physical, sexual or psychological harm or suffering to a woman, in both the public and private spheres.

It's worth pointing out that women don't suffer from just one type of violence, but several types of violence, such as moral, physical and sexual aggression, and that these forms of violence are not restricted to the partner or ex-partner as the main aggressor, but rather family members, friends, acquaintances, strangers and even institutions linked to the state.

2.1.1- Gender Violence:

The anatomical and physiological characteristics associated with biological reproduction refer to sex, while the sexual highs experienced symbolically allude to gender.

It's worth pointing out that these socially accentuated roles of men and women ratify beliefs about the concepts mentioned above, so that differences in conduct, desires and manners are seen as products of biological differences.

It's worth mentioning that sex is simply a biological category to differentiate between men and women based on anatomical differences (penis, breasts and vagina).

Therefore, gender differences are established socially and are subject to how society conceives and visualizes being a woman and a man. Through everyday practices, the designation of the male and female universe is therefore installed, imposing different dispositions of dominance and power.

This violence, based on the difference between the sexes, is what we call gender violence. It is worth mentioning, however, that there is not just one type of violence against women, as we will see below.

2.1.2- Domestic violence and family violence:

Domestic violence is one or more forms of violence practiced in a woman's family and living environment. It takes place in a physical space in which the man dominates the entire territory. People living in this territory, whether or not they have blood ties, owe obedience to this man.

Portraying the spaces of coexistence and relationships, gender violence is defined as family violence, considering the involvement of people from the family nucleus or from the extended family who are related to the victim.

However, when the violence practiced against the woman is by a person who lives with her partially or wholly, but does not belong to her family, it is considered domestic violence.

It is worth noting that even violence that takes place outside the home, but in which the aggressor is a relative, is also considered domestic violence.

Here we can consider domestic violence to be perverse, given that it is practiced on the basis of a woman's emotional bond with her aggressor.

According to the "Map of Violence 2012: Homicide of Women in Brazil", released on June 11, 2012, Brazil ranks 7th among the 84 countries analyzed as having the highest rate of homicide of women. According to the survey, the homicide rate in Brazil was around 4.4 victims per 100,000 women.

When we analyzed documents and bibliographies on the subject of violence against women, we identified three phases that, in general, most women who suffer violence experience, which helps them to remain in this relationship for a longer period of time - this is called the cycle of violence:

1-   Tension: This is the phase when there are intense fights and disagreements, which makes women feel very insecure.

2- Explosion: This is the second phase of the cycle in which the aggressor commits the various forms of violence mentioned below.

3- Honeymoon: The third and final phase of this cycle has this name because it is the moment when the couple reconciles, the aggressor says he is sorry for everything he has done, asks for forgiveness and verbalizes that he will no longer commit such an atrocity.

Below is a graph that illustrates the cycle of violence:

(Source: internet)

It should be emphasized that the name "cycle" is used precisely because there is no change, i.e. both the woman and the aggressor remain in this relationship, and it is important to stress that it takes a short time for the honeymoon phase to return to the tension phase.

However, we would point out that not all women who have suffered violence have actually experienced the phases of the cycle, but it is important to have this knowledge in order to have a good understanding and compression of the majority of women who go through this cycle.

In relation to the types of violence practiced against women, we must understand that although each one has its own concept, they are not practiced in isolation and in a single instance.

Chapter II of Law 11.340-2006, commonly known in Brazil as the "Maria da Penha Law", describes the following types of domestic and family violence against women: physical, psychological, sexual, property and moral violence.

For greater detail and definition, the concept of each of the types of violence mentioned in the law is listed below, starting with Article 7.

2.1.3- - Psychological violence:

It is defined as any conduct that causes emotional harm, impairs and disturbs full development or that aims to degrade or control their actions, behavior, beliefs and decisions, by means of threats, embarrassment, humiliation, manipulation, among others.

This violence is silent and is linked to all the other forms. It is easy to confuse, as it presents itself to women as excessive care and protection.

2.1.4- Physical violence:

It is understood as any conduct that offends their bodily integrity or health.

This type of violence is easy to interpret, as it is visible and leaves marks all over the victim's body due to the use of weapons, slaps, punches, kicks and so on.

2.1.5- Sexual violence:

Any conduct that forces a woman to witness, maintain or participate in unwanted sexual intercourse, through intimidation, threats, coercion or the use of force.

This type of violence is commonly associated with people who are not part of the woman's life, which helps to camouflage it when it is practiced by the woman's partner in the domestic environment.

2.1.6- - Property violence:

This is the case of the retention, subtraction, partial or total destruction of objects, work instruments, personal documents, goods, valuables and rights or economic resources.

This violence occurs when a man limits a woman's right to come and go, when he is driven by a feeling of possession, jealousy towards his wife, for example, and breaks his partner's cell phone, burns her clothes, among other things.

2.1.8- - Moral violence:

It is understood as any conduct that constitutes slander, defamation or libel.

This violence is usually practiced by the boyfriend/girlfriend when comments are made that discredit the woman's conduct through swearing, insinuations, etc.

It is clear that women suffer not just one type of violence, but several, as mentioned above, and that they suffer violence in the public sphere from strangers, even from public institutions, and especially in the domestic family environment, with partners, ex-partners and current partners being the main aggressors.

CHAPTER III - BRIEF ANALYSIS OF THE SOCIAL ASPECTS OF VIOLENCE AGAINST WOMEN

3.1 - Analyzing the social aspects of violence against women:

As mentioned above in Chapter I and also in Chapter II, the concept of gender aims to designate the social construction of men and women, seeking to break with biological determinations.

The way in which the behavior and way of being of men and women is determined is through social and cultural relationships.

In view of this, it is necessary and salutary to understand the socio-historical aspects of discrimination against women in order to denaturalize this type of conduct and treatment towards them.

Male supremacy in relation to the feminine presupposes the subordination and submission of women to men. It is worth noting that the characteristics imposed on women, such as being fragile, loving, caring and delicate, are the opposite of those imposed on men, such as being strong, brave, virile and rational.

Under the guise of the protection that men had to offer women because of their fragility, men obtained from women both collaboration in their work and the submissive behavior that patriarchal family societies have always understood to be a woman's duty in relation to the head of the family (SAFFIOTI, 2013, p.63).

When a woman doesn't fit into these characteristics determined and disseminated in the culture of our society, she in turn suffers criticism of a moralizing and prejudiced nature.

Attitudes that are taken by men in relation to something that is thought to affect their virility and male "honor", they use force and violence to "solve" what may have happened.

When analyzing discourses that are part of everyday social relations, we often come across the following expressions: "she deserved it", "she knows why she's being beaten", "she caused the situation".

Expressions like this lead us to understand that the violence practiced against women in society is a way of punishing and correcting their conduct, which is not in line with what is determined for them.

As a result of social and cultural issues, violence against women stems from economic, social, political and cultural factors that are reproduced in society where, in order to be confirmed, the male appropriates the use of force and violence and the female behaves delicately and docilely.

According to Saffioti (2013, p.85), "The condition of women in class societies has been seen by numerous scholars as the result of the injunction of two kinds of factors: natural and social".

Among the various social aspects of violence against women, in this final coursework, we will briefly discuss the question of whether sexist practices are interconnected with the education offered.

3.1.1- Machismo

Male chauvinism is understood to be a cultural issue that is produced and reproduced at the heart of society through social relationships. Various studies have shown that men sometimes practice violence in order to impose themselves as such.

As already mentioned in this article, the education practiced for both is different, where they are encouraged and guided in their games to use force and aggression to achieve what they want.

It can be considered that violence against women occurs in a dialectical way, where jealousy, the use of alcohol and psychoactive substances become possible reasons for aggression.

However, these social aspects cannot be analyzed in isolation, so it is necessary to understand them analytically in order to denaturalize and remove the process of guilt, because the inequality that is established between the two is also an expression of the social question.

We can reflect on what Iamamoto says about violence as an expression of the social question:

The image of poverty is radicalized: it is the dangerous, the transgressor, the one who steals and doesn't work, subject to repression and extinction. It is the "dangerous classes", and no longer the industrious, who are the target of repression. Institutionalized violence is thus reinforced, putting the right to life itself at risk (IAMAMOTO, 2009, p. 42).

We must be clear and understand that preventing and ending violence against women will not only be achieved through coercion and punishment. We need mechanisms that curb it, but also have the capacity to transform socio-cultural relations and really understand that men and women have the same rights and duties in society.

Therefore, in the following chapter, we will look at and discuss public policies, treaties, among others, that show us what is being done as a mechanism to care for women in situations of violence, as well as other practices pertinent to the phenomenon mentioned above.

CHAPTER IV - TREATY CONVENTIONS AND THE MARIA DA PENHA LAW

We can see that throughout human history, women have been stigmatized as those who should provide care and be inferior to male potential.

Thinking about violence against women and considering it to be the result of socially unequal relations between men and women, here are some treaties and conventions that deserve attention in the fight against violence against women.

It is worth highlighting once again the participation and militancy of the feminist movement at conferences, forums and in discussions with the state to put public policies into effect.

As such, we cannot fail to point out that the 1988 Federal Constitution, when it was promulgated, made progress in relation to women, with Article 226 and its 5th paragraphs standing out, where it "broke" the marital headship that until then only included the man as being responsible for the family and from then on dealt with rights and duties in relation to society as being shared equally.

Paragraph 6 points out that civil marriage can be dissolved by divorce, so a woman has the right to freedom when the relationship is no longer compatible with her wishes.

The first treaty on violence against women, approved by the UN through resolution 34/180 of December 18, 1979, was the "Convention on the Elimination of All Forms of Discrimination Against Women", but it was only in the 1980s, more precisely in 1984, that it came into force, broadly presenting women's human rights.

It presents the promotion of women's human rights with a view to gender equality and, therefore, to curbing any form of violation and discrimination against women.

In 1993, the world conference on human rights took place in Vienna, Austria, and activists from the feminist movement took a stand saying: "Human rights are also women's rights", which can be achieved by including the fact that the human rights of women and children are inalienable and form part of universal human rights.

All this gave rise to the "Inter-American Convention on the Prevention, Punishment and Eradication of Violence against Women". It is important to note that this convention defines the issue of gender-based violence as a set of other forms of violence and reinforces that it is not only linked to the private sphere, i.e. in any space where women live and suffer some form of violence, it is considered to be violence caused by unequal gender relations and treatment.

In 1995, the Fourth World Conference on Women's Rights was held in Bejim. At this conference, women's human rights were definitively recognized in action and in the declaration.

The 1994 Inter-American Convention on the Prevention, Punishment and Eradication of Violence against Women, then known as the "Convention of Belém do Parà", provides a clear definition of what is understood to be violence against women, the places where types of violence occur, reinforcing that it is a violation of human rights and linking the issue of gender as the foundation of violence against women. Brazil approved and ratified the Belém do Parà Convention in 1995.

Article 2 of the Belém do Parà Convention states:

Violence against women is understood to include physical, sexual and psychological violence:

1- That has occurred within the family or domestic unit or in any interpersonal relationship in which the aggressor lives or has lived in the same household as the woman and includes, among others, rape, rape, ill-treatment and sexual abuse;

2- That has occurred in the community and is perpetrated by any person and includes, among others, rape, sexual abuse, torture, ill-treatment of persons, trafficking in women, forced prostitution, kidnapping and sexual harassment in the workplace, as well as in educational institutions, health facilities or any other place, and

3- That is perpetrated or tolerated by the state or its agents, wherever it occurs (Belém do Para Convention, 1995).

The high level of violence practiced against women, especially in the domestic family space, and with the struggle and resistance of the feminist movement, reached a fundamental legislative milestone, Law No. 11.340/2006, commonly known as the Maria da Penha Law, which was sanctioned on August 7, 2006 by the then President of the Republic Luiz Inâcio Lula da Silva, it is important to note that this law became known by the name Maria da Penha, in honor of the Ceará biopharmacist Maria da Penha Maia.

It is important to mention that this law was based on article 226, paragraph 8 of the 1988 Federal Constitution, the Inter-American Convention on the Prevention, Punishment and Eradication of Violence against Women, the Convention on the Elimination of All Forms of Violence against Women and international treaties signed by the Brazilian government with a view to creating mechanisms to curb domestic and family violence against women.

Law 11.340/2006 provides for and institutes the creation of special courts for the crimes provided for in that law, establishes public policies aimed at women, ratifying their rights and also measures to protect and assist women in situations of violence.

The Maria da Penha law prohibits the payment of baskets of food and pecuniary penalties, establishes that special courts can count on multidisciplinary teams from the psychosocial, legal and health areas, and determines the creation of a national system of data and statistics on domestic violence.

It is worth noting that with this law society has made great progress in relation to violence in the domestic and family sphere, as well as breaking with the legal view of crimes committed against women as irrelevant criminal offenses. In relation to the Brazilian Penal Code and Criminal Procedure Code, this law made changes to the treatment of crimes committed against women.

However, Law 11.340/2006 is subject to criticism and different understandings in relation to its discriminatory application, which does not take into account the situation of women in society, analyzing it from a social perspective, given that it is the result of a patriarchal culture.

The resolutions adopted and Law 11.340/2006 in the Brazilian case can be considered an expression of the resistance of women who recognize violence against them and question biological or even domestic explanations.

They treat it as a gender issue that results from a process of historical and social construction involving a set of social values. In other words, these values show and define the rules of behavior expected and practiced by men and women, even in contemporary societies.

These treaties, laws and conventions were conceived and articulated with the aim of achieving gender equality between the rights of women and men, since they dealt with the issue of human rights in a generalized way.

Summarizing only the criticisms related to it, the law establishes a new legal order in the country in relation to women in situations of violence, but we still have many women even after 10 years of promulgation of the law who are still unaware of the guarantees brought by the law, or the fear of breaking the silence and becoming a fatal victim of the aggressor.

4.1 - Brazilian social policies and mechanisms to combat violence against women

The first police station for women in situations of violence was set up in 1985 in the state of São Paulo, the same year that the National Council for Women's Rights (CNDM) was created.

Later that year, the first shelter for women at risk of death was also created in São Paulo. It is worth pointing out that these three major achievements for Brazilian women were the result of militancy on the part of the feminist movement, pushing the state to do its part in proposing and implementing actions aimed at the population, in this case women in situations of violence.

Between 1985 and 2002, these services were the main focus of policies to combat violence against women, with an emphasis on public security and social assistance.

In 2003, with the creation of the Secretariat for Women's Policies (SPM), new actions were taken to combat violence against women, such as reference centers for women's services, women's defense offices, and the construction of a women's service network.

With the national women's conference in 2004, the national plan for women's policies was created, which in turn points out that the responsibility for assisting women who suffer violence is not restricted to the actions of social assistance and public security policies, as this phenomenon involves all public policies in terms of action and responsibility.

In 2005, the federal government set up a call center for women in situations of violence, which aims to help and guide women in cases of violence by dialing 180. Calls are free and the service is available 24 hours a day, including weekends and public holidays.

The services focused on assisting women in situations of domestic violence are organized and named by the Secretariat for Women's Policy (SPM) as the network for combating violence against women, the concept of which is defined by the SPM itself:

"articulated action between governmental and non-governmental institutions and services, as well as the community, with a view to developing effective protection strategies and policies aimed at guaranteeing the empowerment of women and their human rights, as well as the accountability of aggressors and qualified assistance to these women who, for the time being, find themselves in a situation of violence."

The care network, on the other hand, refers to the set of actions and services from different sectors, especially in relation to the social assistance policy, the justice system, health and public security.

These services aim to expand and improve the quality of care, to identify and provide appropriate referrals to all women in situations of violence, to protect their integrity and, finally, to humanize care.

Therefore, in the services that assist women in situations of violence, the process of welcoming and <u>qualified listening is </u>of the utmost importance (my emphasis). In this process, the professional team will demonstrate to the woman that they are ready to meet her demands, give importance to her situation and provide the appropriate referrals and other procedures that should be taken.

With qualified listening, it is possible to convey a service of trust and support to the woman, as well as allowing the professional to identify the situation of violence in which the woman finds herself.

In 2013, President Dilma Rousseff launched the "Women, Living without Violence" program, with the aim of expanding and integrating all the public services aimed at women in situations of violence in a way that articulates specialized services in the fields of justice, health, the social assistance network and public security, among others. This strategy was transformed into a program by Decree 8.086 of August 30, 2013.

The SPM is responsible for coordinating the program and its implementation is coordinated by the Ministries of Health, Justice, Labor and Employment and Social Development and Fight against Hunger.

Between the year of its launch and 2014, with the exception of the state of Pernambuco, 26 states signed up to the Women: Living Without Violence program.

The program's lines of action are structured as follows:

Implementation of the Brazilian women's house, expansion of the women's call centre - call 180, organization and humanization of care for victims of sexual violence, implementation and maintenance of women's care centers in dry border regions, ongoing awareness campaigns, mobile units to assist women in situations of violence in the countryside and forest.

The documentary research carried out in this chapter on the services and programs created since the Maria da Penha law was enacted shows that the public authorities have tried to respond to the problem of violence against women.

However, one cannot fail to mention the tireless and persistent militancy of social movements, especially the feminist movement, which is present and active in all spheres and spaces for deliberating actions on the issue of women in situations of violence in this country.

FINAL CONSIDERATIONS

The concept of gender has played an important role in the bibliographical and documentary work presented here. As a category of analysis, it has been a fundamental theoretical reference for studies of the situation of violence practiced against women, leading us to understand the social inequalities in a society where it is proclaimed that the masculine is preponderant and fundamental.

It is worth highlighting the struggles of the feminist social movements over the years, which have played a fundamental role in guaranteeing and seeking the realization and recognition of women's rights.

It is important to point out that the field of social public policies geared towards the issue of violence against women has made considerable progress, but there is still a daily struggle to make what has already been achieved a reality and to improve other areas of care for women in situations of violence.

The Maria da Penha Law is considered to be a major milestone in the fight to end violence against women. It is an instrument for protecting women who are victims of domestic violence, since it unites the three spheres of power and guarantees the reduction and prevention of cases of this type of violence.

However, in addition to decrees, laws and policies focused on assisting women in situations of violence and punishing the aggressor, it is necessary to invest in universal social and cultural policies to act as educational and preventive practices that start with schooling and are perpetuated in society.

This means that public authorities must make an ethical and political commitment to multi-professional teams, as well as training and continuing education to systematically attend to and monitor the expressions of violence against women.

And that civil society corroborates, through discussion spaces (councils), the adoption of public policies aimed at assisting victims of violence on an ongoing basis, never losing sight of the need to develop educational, economic and cultural public policies that, in fact, contribute to the reduction of social and gender inequalities and, in turn, help to build equal relationships between women and men.

BIBLIOGRAPHICAL REFERENCES

BEAUVOIR, Simone. *The Second Sex*. 4ª Ed. Sao Paulo: Difusao Européia do Livro, 1970.

BRAZIL. **Federal Constitution 1988.** 39th edition updated in 2013.

. Presidency of the Republic. Office of the Chief of Staff. **Law 11.3040-2006** - "Maria da Penha Law"

. Presidency of the Republic. **Decree no. 8.086, of August 30, 2013.**

. SPECIAL SECRETARIAT FOR WOMEN'S POLICIES - SPM. **Network to Combat Violence against Women**. Brasilia/DF, 2011.

. **National policy to combat violence against women**. Brasilia-DF 2011.

BUTLER, Judith. **Gender Trouble: feminism and the subversion of identity.** Ed: Civilizaçao Brasileira. Rio de Janeiro, 2003.

CARNEIRO. Alessandra Acosta and FRAGA. Cristina Kologeski. **The Maria da Penha Law: from reported violence to silenced violence.** In: Revista Serviço Social & Sociedade n. 110 - Sao Paulo: Cortez, 2012.

Convention of Belém do Parà Adopted by the General Assembly of the Organization of American States on June 6, 1994 - ratified by Brazil on November 27, 1995

Women's rights. Sao Paulo: Editora Melhoramentos, 2011. (your rights)

Engels, Friedrich. **The Origin of the Family, Private Property and the State.** Sao Paulo: Escala Educacional, 2009.

HALL, Stuart. **A identidade cultura na pós-modernidade;** traduçao Tomaz Tadeu da Silva, Guaracira Lopes Louro. 11th Ed. Rio de Janeiro: DP&A, 2006.

IAMAMOTO, Marilda Vilela and CARVALHO, Raul. **Social Relations and Social Service in Brazil: Outline of a historical-methodological interpretation.** 28ª edition. Sâo Paulo:

Editora Cortez, 2009.

MIGUEL, Luis Felipe. Biroli Flavia. **Feminism and Politics** - 1st ed. - Sâo Paulo: Boitempo, 2014.

MINAYO. Maria Cecilia de Souza; DESLANDES, Suely Ferreira; GOMES, Romeu. **Pesquisa social.** 29a.Ed. Rio de Janeiro: Vozes, 2010.

PERROT, Michele. **Public Women.** Sâo Paulo: Fundaçâo Editora da UNESP, 1998.

Prefeitura Municipal de Sâo Paulo, Coordenadoria da Mulher - **Guia de Procedimentos para atendimento a mulheres em situaçâo de violência nos centros de referência de atendimento a mulher e nos centros de cidadania da mulher.**

WOMEN'S NETWORK. **Fighting for Women's Rights**. Available at: <http://www.redemulher.org.br/luta.htm>.

SAFFIOTI, Heleieth I. B. **Women in Class Society**: Myth and Reality. Expressâo popular. 2013.

. **Gender, Patriarchy, Violence**. Sâo Paulo: Ed. Fundaçâo Perseu Abramo, 2004.

. **A lógica do Galinheiro**.In: Violência em debate. p.39-57, Sâo Paulo: Moderna, 1997.

SCHAIBER, Lilia B lima. [ET AL.] - **Violence hurts and is not a right: violence against women, health and human rights.** Sâo Paulo: Editora UNESP, 2005.

SCOTT, Joan W. **The enigma of equality**. Rev. Estud. Fem., Florianópolis, v.13, n.1, abr. 2005. Available at: <http://www.scielo.br/scielo

SILVA. Marlise Vinagre. **Violence against women: Who scoops it up^** - Sao Paulo: Cortez, 1992.

SOUZA. Bruna Tavares. **REFLECTIONS ON THE SOCIAL ASPECTS OF DOMESTIC VIOLENCE AGAINST WOMEN.** Course Conclusion Paper defended in the Social Work course at the Fluminense Federal University - Rio das Ostras University Campus. March

2013.

SOUZA, Ednilsa R. de. **Social Violence: a challenge for public health services.** In: Saùde em foco, n° 13, p. 2-3, Secretaria Municipal de Saùde, Rio de Janeiro, 1996.

TELES, Maria Amélia de Almeida; MELO, Monica. **What is violence against women.** Sao Paulo: Brasiliense, 2012.

Waiselfisz, Julio Jacobo. Map of Violence 2012**. The new patterns of homicidal violence in Brazil.** Sao Paulo, Sangari Institute, 2011

INTERNET

http://www.spm.gov.br/assuntos/violencia/programa-mulher-viver-sem-violencia   accessed on August 23, 2015 at 2:24 p.m.

ANNEX 1

When we analyze some Brazilian songs, we can see in funks, pagodas, forrós, lyrics that depreciate the condition of the female gender in our society, reinforcing the condition of women as subordinate and submissive to "macho" men, reinforcing the issue of violent practices towards women.

This shows us how much we have to look for alternatives to change this paradigm that is ingrained in our daily lives and in the relationship practices between women and men. For a better illustration, I present below a forró group's lyrics:

Kneel and weep

Tradition Group

Composition: Luiz Clàudio/ Maruinhos Ulian/ Sandro Coelho

I was tired of playing the good guy

Calling you bendy,

Of love and mistress

This evil woman used me and snubbed me

And he was very mean to me

I got tough and decided to play the macho man

That's good

And now it's my way

From now on

Whenever I call you

I think you should kneel

And treat me with respect.

2x refrain

Kneel down and cry

Kneel down and cry

The more I tie the bow

Much more she loves me

But the effect of the medicine I gave

It was better than I thought

She does whatever I want.

Do laundry, wash dishes,

Looking after the children

Ride the rails

This woman has come into her own

Cuddle,

Hold me close

Call me sweetie

I started to worry

And I'm thinking that this crazy woman

She got used to it

And he's enjoying being beaten

ANNEX 2

Presidency of the Republic

Civil House

Legal Affairs Bureau

<u>LAW NO. 11.340, OF AUGUST 7, 2006.</u>

Creates mechanisms to curb domestic and family violence against women, under the terms of § 8º of art. 226 of the Federal Constitution, the Convention on the Elimination of All Forms of Discrimination against Women and the Inter-American Convention on the Prevention, Punishment and Eradication of Violence against Women; provides for the creation of Domestic and Family Violence Courts against Women; amends the Code of Criminal Procedure, the Criminal Code and the Criminal Execution Law; and makes other provisions.

THE PRESIDENT OF THE REPUBLIC I hereby make known that the National Congress decrees and I sanction the following Law:

TITLE I

PRELIMINARY PROVISIONS

Art. 1 This Law creates mechanisms to curb and prevent domestic and family violence against women, under the terms of <u>§ 8º of Art. 226 of the Federal Constitution</u>, the Convention on the Elimination of All Forms of Violence against Women, the Inter-American Convention on the Prevention, Punishment and Eradication of Violence against Women and other international treaties ratified by the Federative Republic of Brazil; provides for the creation of Domestic and Family Violence Courts against Women; and establishes measures to assist and protect women in situations of domestic and family violence.

Every woman, regardless of class, race, ethnicity, sexual orientation, income, culture, educational level, age and religion, enjoys the fundamental rights inherent to the human person, and is guaranteed the opportunities and facilities to live without violence, preserve her physical and mental health and her moral, intellectual and social development.

Art. 3: Women will be guaranteed the conditions for the effective exercise of the rights to life, security, health, food, education, culture, housing, access to justice, sport, leisure, work, citizenship, freedom, dignity, respect and family and community life.

§ 1º Public authorities shall develop policies aimed at guaranteeing women's human rights in domestic and family relations, in order to protect them from all forms of neglect, discrimination, exploitation, violence, cruelty and oppression.

§ Paragraph 2 - It is up to the family, society and public authorities to create the necessary conditions for the effective exercise of the rights set out in the caput.

Art. 4º In interpreting this Law, the social purposes for which it is intended and, in particular, the specific conditions of women in situations of domestic and family violence shall be taken into account.

TiTLE II

DOMESTIC AND FAMILY VIOLENCE AGAINST WOMEN

CHAPTER I

GENERAL PROVISIONS

Art. 5º For the purposes of this Law, any action or omission based on gender that causes death, injury, physical, sexual or psychological suffering and moral or property damage constitutes domestic and family violence against women: (See Complementary Law No. 150 of 2015)

I   - within the domestic unit, understood as the permanent living space of people, with or without family ties, including those sporadically added;

II   - within the family, understood as the community formed by individuals who are or consider themselves related, united by natural ties, affinity or express will;

III   - in any intimate relationship of affection in which the aggressor lives or has lived with the victim, regardless of cohabitation

Sole paragraph. The personal relationships listed in this article are independent of sexual orientation.

Art. 6º Domestic and family violence against women is a form of human rights violation.

CHAPTER II

FORMS OF DOMESTIC AND FAMILY VIOLENCE

AGAINST WOMEN

Art. 7º These are forms of domestic and family violence against women, among others:

IV   - physical violence, understood as any conduct that offends their bodily integrity or health;

V   I - psychological violence, understood as any conduct that causes emotional harm and diminished self-esteem or that harms and disturbs full development or that aims to degrade or control their actions, behaviors, beliefs and decisions, through threat, embarrassment, humiliation, manipulation, isolation, constant surveillance, constant persecution, insult, blackmail, ridicule, exploitation and limitation of the right to come and go, or any other means that cause harm to their psychological health and self-determination;

VI   I - sexual violence, understood as any conduct that forces her to witness, maintain or participate in an unwanted sexual relationship, through intimidation, threat, coercion or use of force; that induces her to commercialize or use her sexuality in any way, that prevents her from using any contraceptive method or that forces her into marriage, pregnancy, abortion or prostitution, through coercion, blackmail, bribery or manipulation; or that limits or annuls the exercise of her sexual and reproductive rights;

VII   - property violence, understood as any conduct that involves the retention, removal, partial or total destruction of their objects, work tools, personal documents, goods, values and rights or economic resources, including those intended to satisfy their needs;

VIII   - moral violence, understood as any conduct that constitutes slander, defamation or insult.

TiTLE III

ASSISTANCE TO WOMEN IN SITUATIONS OF DOMESTIC AND FAMILY VIOLENCE

CHAPTER I

INTEGRATED PREVENTION MEASURES

Art. 8 - The public policy aimed at curbing domestic and family violence against women will be carried out by means of an articulated set of actions by the Union, the States, the Federal District and the Municipalities, as well as non-governmental actions, with the following guidelines:

I   - the operational integration of the Judiciary, the Public Prosecutor's Office and the Public Defender's Office with the areas of public security, social assistance, health, education, work and housing;

II   - the promotion of studies and research, statistics and other relevant information, from the perspective of gender and race or ethnicity, concerning the causes, consequences and frequency of domestic and family violence against women, for the systematization of data, to be unified nationally, and the periodic evaluation of the results of the measures adopted;

III   - respect, in the media, for the ethical and social values of the individual and the family, in order to curb stereotyped roles that legitimize or exacerbate domestic and family violence, in accordance with the provisions of <u>item III of art. 1º</u>, <u>item IV of art. 3º</u> and <u>item IV of art. 221 of the Federal Constitution</u>;

IV   - the implementation of specialized police assistance for women, particularly in the Women's Police Stations;

V   - the promotion and implementation of educational campaigns to prevent domestic and family violence against women, aimed at schoolchildren and society in general, and the dissemination of this Law and the instruments for the protection of women's human rights;

VI   - the signing of agreements, protocols, adjustments, terms or other instruments to promote partnerships between government bodies or between them and non-governmental entities, with the aim of implementing programs to eradicate domestic and family violence against women;

VII   - the permanent training of the Civil and Military Police, the Municipal Guard, the Fire Brigade and the professionals belonging to the bodies and areas listed in item I with regard to gender and race or ethnicity issues;

VIII   - the promotion of educational programs that disseminate ethical values of unrestricted respect for the dignity of the human person from the perspective of gender and race or ethnicity;

IX   - the emphasis in school curricula at all levels of education on content relating to human rights, gender and racial or ethnic equity and the problem of domestic and family violence against women.

CHAPTER II

ASSISTANCE TO WOMEN IN SITUATIONS OF DOMESTIC AND FAMILY VIOLENCE

Art. 9º Assistance to women in situations of domestic and family violence will be provided in an articulated manner and in accordance with the principles and guidelines laid down in the Organic Law on Social Assistance, the Unified Health System, the Unified Public Security System, among other public protection norms and policies, and on an emergency basis where appropriate.

§ 1º The judge will order, for a certain period of time, the inclusion of women in situations of domestic and family violence in the register of assistance programs of the federal, state and municipal governments.

§ 2º The judge will ensure that women in situations of domestic and family violence have physical and psychological integrity:

I   - priority access to removal when she is a public servant, part of the direct or indirect administration;

II   - maintenance of the employment relationship, when it is necessary to leave the workplace for up to six months.

§ 30   Assistance to women in situations of domestic and family violence will include access to the benefits arising from scientific and technological development, including emergency contraception services, prophylaxis of Sexually Transmitted Diseases (STDs) and Acquired Immune Deficiency Syndrome (AIDS) and other necessary and appropriate medical procedures in cases of sexual violence.

CHAPTER III

ATTENDANCE BY THE POLICE AUTHORITY

Art. 10: In the event of imminent or actual domestic and family violence against women, the police authority that becomes aware of the occurrence will immediately take the appropriate legal measures.

Sole paragraph. The provisions of the caput of this article shall apply to non-compliance with a granted emergency protective measure.

Art. 11: When assisting women in situations of domestic and family violence, the police authority shall, among other measures:

I   - guarantee police protection when necessary, immediately informing the Public Prosecutor's Office and the Judiciary;

II   - take the victim to a hospital or health center and to the Forensic Medical Institute;

III   - provide transportation for the victim and their dependents to a shelter or safe place, when there is a risk to their life;

IV   - if necessary, accompany the victim to ensure that her belongings are removed from the scene or from the family home;

V   - inform the victim of her rights under this law and the services available.

Art. 12: In all cases of domestic and family violence against women, once the incident has been registered, the police authority shall immediately adopt the following procedures, without prejudice to those provided for in the Code of Criminal Procedure:

I   - listen to the offended party, draw up the police report and make a final statement, if presented;

II   - gather all the evidence needed to clarify the fact and its circumstances;

III   - within 48 (forty-eight) hours, send a separate file to the judge with the victim's request for emergency protective measures;

IV   - order a forensic examination of the victim and request other necessary forensic examinations;

V   - hear the aggressor and the witnesses;

VI   - order the identification of the aggressor and have his criminal record attached to the case file, indicating the existence of an arrest warrant or other police record against him;

VII   - send the police investigation files to the judge and the Public Prosecutor's Office within the legal time limit.

§ 1º The offended woman's request will be taken down by the police authority and must contain:

I   - qualification of the victim and the aggressor;

II   - name and age of dependents;

III   - a brief description of the incident and the protective measures requested by the victim.

§ Paragraph 2 The police authority shall attach the police report and a copy of all available documents in the possession of the victim to the document referred to in paragraph 1.

§ Paragraph 3 Medical reports or records provided by hospitals and health centers will be admitted as evidence.

TiTLE IV

THE PROCEDURES

CHAPTER I

GENERAL PROVISIONS

Art 13: The rules of the Codes of Criminal Procedure and Civil Proceduro and tho cpooifio logiolation roloting to children, adolescents and the elderly that do not conflict with the provisions of this Law shall apply to the prosecution, judgment and execution of civil and criminal cases arising from the practice of domestic and family violence against women.

Art. 14: The Courts of Domestic and Family Violence against Women, bodies of ordinary justice with civil and criminal jurisdiction, may be created by the Union, in the Federal District and Territories, and by the States, for the prosecution, judgment and execution of cases arising from the practice of domestic and family violence against women.

Sole paragraph. Procedural acts may take place at night, in accordance with the rules of judicial organization.

Art. 15: At the option of the victim, the Court has jurisdiction over civil cases governed by this Law:

I   - of your domicile or residence;

II   - of the place of the event on which the claim is based;

III   - of the aggressor's home.

Art. 16: In the public criminal actions subject to the representation of the offended party referred to in this Law, the waiver of representation shall only be admitted before the judge, at a hearing specially appointed for this purpose, before the complaint is received and the Public Prosecutor's Office is heard.

Art. 17: In cases of domestic and family violence against women, it is forbidden to apply sentences of a food basket or other monetary payments, as well as the substitution of a sentence that implies the payment of a fine in isolation.

CHAPTER II

EMERGENCY PROTECTIVE MEASURES

Section I

General Provisions

Art. 18: Once the case file with the offended party's request has been received, the judge shall, within 48 (forty-eight) hours:

I - to examine the case file and the request and decide on emergency protective measures;

II - order the victim to be referred to the legal aid agency, where appropriate;

III - inform the Public Prosecutor's Office so that it can take the appropriate measures.

Art. 19: Emergency protective measures may be granted by the judge at the request of the Public Prosecutor's Office or at the request of the victim.

§ 1º Emergency protective measures may be granted immediately, regardless of the parties' hearing or the Public Prosecutor's Office's manifestation, and the latter must be promptly notified.

§ Paragraph 2 The emergency protective measures will be applied individually or cumulatively, and may be replaced at any time by others that are more effective, whenever the rights recognized in this Law are threatened or violated.

§ 30   The judge may, at the request of the Public Prosecutor's Office or at the request of the victim, grant new emergency protective measures or review those already granted, if he deems it necessary to protect the victim, her family and her property, after hearing the Public Prosecutor's Office.

Art. 20: At any stage of the police investigation or criminal investigation, the aggressor may be remanded in custody, decreed by the judge, ex officio, at the request of the Public Prosecutor's Office or upon representation by the police authority.

Sole paragraph. The judge may revoke pre-trial detention if, in the course of the proceedings, he finds that there is no reason for it to continue, or he may re-declare it if reasons arise to justify it.

Art. 21: The victim must be notified of procedural acts concerning the aggressor, especially those pertaining to entering and leaving prison, without prejudice to the notification of the lawyer or public defender.

Sole paragraph. The victim may not deliver any summons or notification to the aggressor.

Section II

Urgent Protective Measures that Oblige the Aggressor

Art. 22: If domestic and family violence against women is found to have been committed under the terms of this Law, the judge may immediately apply the following emergency protective measures to the aggressor, either jointly or separately, among others:

I   - suspension of possession or restriction of carrying weapons, with notification to the competent body, under the terms of Law No. 10.826, of December 22, 2003;

II   - removal from the home, domicile or place of cohabitation with the victim;

III   - prohibition of certain conducts, including:

a)   approaching the victim, her family and witnesses, setting a minimum distance between them and the aggressor;

b)   contact with the victim, her family and witnesses by any means of communication;

c)   frequentation of certain places in order to preserve the physical and psychological integrity of the victim;

IV   - restriction or suspension of visits to minor dependents, after hearing the multidisciplinary care team or similar service;

V   - provision of provisional or interim maintenance.

§ 10   The measures referred to in this article do not prevent the application of other measures provided for in current legislation, whenever the safety of the victim or the circumstances so require, and the measure must be communicated to the Public Prosecutor's Office.

§ 2º   In the event of the application of item I, if the aggressor is in the conditions mentioned in the <u>heading and items of art. 6º of Law no. 10.826, of December 22, 2003</u>, the judge will notify the respective body, corporation or institution of the emergency protective measures granted and will order the restriction of the carrying of weapons, with the aggressor's immediate superior being responsible for complying with the judicial order, under penalty of incurring the crimes of prevarication or disobedience, as the case may be.

§ 3º   In order to guarantee the effectiveness of emergency protective measures, the judge may request police assistance at any time.

§ 4º   The provisions of the caput and <u>§§ 5º and 6 of Article 461 of Law No. 5.869, of January 11, 1973 (Code of Civil Procedure)</u> shall apply to the cases provided for in this article, where applicable.

Section III

Urgent Protective Measures for the Victim

Art. 23: The judge may, when necessary, without prejudice to other measures:

I   - refer the victim and their dependents to an official or community protection or care program;

II   - order the return of the victim and her dependents to their respective homes, after the aggressor has been removed;

III   - order the removal of the offended party from the home, without prejudice to rights relating to property, custody of children and maintenance;

IV   - order the separation of bodies.

Art. 24: In order to protect the assets of the marital partnership or those privately owned by the woman, the judge may order the following measures, among others:

I   - restitution of property unduly taken by the aggressor from the victim;

II   - temporary prohibition on the conclusion of acts and contracts for the purchase, sale and rental of jointly owned property, unless expressly authorized by the courts;

III   - suspension of the powers of attorney granted by the victim to the aggressor;

IV   - provision of provisional security, by means of a court deposit, for material losses and damages resulting from the practice of domestic and family violence against the victim.

Sole Paragraph. The judge must notify the competent registry office for the purposes set out in items II and III of this article.

CHAPTER III

THE ROLE OF THE PUBLIC PROSECUTOR'S OFFICE

Art. 25: The Public Prosecutor's Office will intervene, when it is not a party, in civil and criminal cases arising from domestic and family violence against women.

Art. 26: The Public Prosecutor's Office, without prejudice to other attributions, shall be responsible for cases of domestic and family violence against women, when necessary:

I   - request police force and public health, education, social assistance and security services, among others;

II   - monitor public and private establishments that provide care for women in situations of domestic and family violence, and immediately adopt the appropriate administrative or judicial measures with regard to any irregularities found;

III   - register cases of domestic and family violence against women.

CHAPTER IV

LEGAL AID

Art. 27: In all procedural acts, civil and criminal, women in situations of domestic and family violence must be accompanied by a lawyer, except as provided for in art. 19 of this Law.

Art. 28: Every woman in a situation of domestic and family violence is guaranteed access to the services of the Public Defender's Office or Free Legal Aid, under the terms of the law, at police and judicial headquarters, through specific and humanized care.

TiTLE V

THE MULTIDISCIPLINARY CARE TEAM

Art. 29: The Domestic and Family Violence Courts that are created may have a multidisciplinary service team, made up of professionals specialized in the psychosocial, legal and health areas.

Art. 30 - It is the responsibility of the multidisciplinary care team, among other duties reserved for it by local legislation, to provide written subsidies to the judge, the Public Prosecutor's Office and the Public Defender's Office, by means of reports or verbally at hearings, and to carry out guidance, referral, prevention and other measures aimed at the victim, the aggressor and their families, with special attention to children and adolescents.

Art. 31: When the complexity of the case requires a more in-depth assessment, the judge may order the opinion of a specialized professional, as indicated by the multidisciplinary care team.

Art. 32: The Judiciary, when drawing up its budget proposal, may provide resources for the creation and maintenance of the multidisciplinary care team, under the terms of the Budget Guidelines Law.

TiTLE VI

TRANSITIONAL PROVISIONS

Art. 33: Until the Domestic and Family Violence Courts against Women are structured, the criminal courts will accumulate civil and criminal jurisdiction to hear and judge cases arising from the practice of domestic and family violence against women, observing the provisions of Title IV of this Law, subsidized by the relevant procedural legislation.

Sole Paragraph. The right of first refusal shall be guaranteed in the criminal courts for the prosecution and judgment of the cases referred to in the heading.

TiTLE VII

FINAL PROVISIONS

Art. 34: The establishment of the Domestic and Family Violence Courts against Women may be accompanied by the implementation of the necessary curatorships and legal aid services.

Art. 35: The Union, the Federal District, the States and the Municipalities may create and promote, within the limits of their respective powers:

I   - comprehensive and multidisciplinary care centers for women and their dependents in situations of domestic and family violence;

II   - shelters for women and their minor dependents in situations of domestic and family violence;

III   - police stations, public defenders' offices, health services and medical-legal examination centers specialized in assisting women in situations of domestic and family violence;

IV   - programs and campaigns to combat domestic and family violence;

V   - education and rehabilitation centers for aggressors.

Art. 36: The Union, the States, the Federal District and the Municipalities shall promote the adaptation of their agencies and programs to the guidelines and principles of this Law.

Art. 37: The defense of trans-individual interests and rights provided for in this Law may be exercised concurrently by the Public Prosecutor's Office and by associations working in the area, regularly constituted for at least one year, under the terms of civil legislation.

Sole paragraph. The requirement of pre-constitution may be waived by the judge when he considers that there is no other entity with adequate representation to file the collective claim.

Art. 38: Statistics on domestic and family violence against women will be included in the databases of the official bodies of the Justice and Security System in order to subsidize the national data and information system for women.

Sole Paragraph. The Public Security Secretariats of the States and the Federal District may send their criminal information to the Ministry of Justice's database.

Art. 39: The Union, the States, the Federal District and the Municipalities, within the limits of their powers and under the terms of their respective budget guidelines laws, may establish specific budget allocations, in each financial year, for the implementation of the measures established in this Law.

Art. 40: The obligations provided for in this Law do not exclude others arising from the principles it adopts.

Art. 41: Law 9.099 of September 26, 1995 does not apply to crimes committed with domestic and family violence against women, regardless of the penalty.

Art. 42 - Art. 313 of Decree-Law No. 3.689, of October 3, 1941 (Code of Criminal Procedure), shall come into force with the addition of the following item IV:

"Art. 313 ....

IV - if the crime involves domestic and family violence against women, under the terms of the specific law, to guarantee the execution of emergency protective measures." (NR)

Art. 43: Point f of item II of art. 61 of Decree-Law no. 2.848, of December 7, 1940 (Penal Code), shall come into force with the following wording:

"Art. 61 ....

II -

f) with abuse of authority or taking advantage of domestic relations, cohabitation or hospitality, or with violence against women in the form of the specific law;

    " ....(NR)

Art. 44: Art. 129 of Decree-Law No. 2848, of December 7, 1940 (Penal Code), shall come into force with the following changes:

"Art. 129 ....

§ Paragraph 9: If the injury is committed against an ascendant, descendant, sibling, spouse or partner, or with whom the perpetrator lives or has lived together, or if the perpetrator takes advantage of domestic relations, cohabitation or hospitality:

Penalty - imprisonment from 3 (three) months to 3 (three) years.

§ In the event of § 9 of this article, the penalty shall be increased by one third if the crime is committed against a disabled person." (NR)

Art. 45: Art. 152 of Law No.º 7.210, of July 11, 1984 (the Penal Execution Law), shall come into force with the following wording:

"Art. 152 ....

Sole paragraph. In cases of domestic violence against women, the judge may order the perpetrator to attend rehabilitation and re-education programs." (NR)

Art. 46 This Law shall enter into force 45 (forty-five) days after its publication.

Brasilia, August 7, 2006; 185th of Independence and 118th of the Republic.

LUIZ INACIO LULA DA SILVA

Dilma Rousseff

This text does not replace the one published in the D.O.U. of 8.8.2006

I want morebooks!

Buy your books fast and straightforward online - at one of world's fastest growing online book stores! Environmentally sound due to Print-on-Demand technologies.

Buy your books online at
www.morebooks.shop

Kaufen Sie Ihre Bücher schnell und unkompliziert online – auf einer der am schnellsten wachsenden Buchhandelsplattformen weltweit! Dank Print-On-Demand umwelt- und ressourcenschonend produziert.

Bücher schneller online kaufen
www.morebooks.shop

Printed by Books on Demand GmbH, Norderstedt / Germany